NORTHERN LIGHTS

By Yukiko Nishimura

*N*orthern Lights is a stunning piece written by Yukiko Nishimura, which weaves together individual musical lines creating a beautiful texture and sonority. This piece captures the visual beauty of the luminous phenomenon, which makes for a spectacular image floating in the sky. The waves of light are similar to the waveform of sound frequencies, and these linear musical lines depict that concept in music. This is a spectacular work that will captivate your students.

Northern Lights is another name for the aurora borealis. I have yet to actually see it myself, but I wanted to express how this beautiful, luminous phenomenon becomes a spectacular image and floats in the sky. The waves of light are similar to the waveform of sound frequencies. Layers of light become layers of sound, floating in slightly different forms in each part. Every part has its own melodic line. Listen to the sounds of the other parts and how they all interact with each other.

Instrumentation

1 — Conductor Score	2 — 1st F Horn	**SUPPLEMENTAL and WORLD PARTS**
5 — 1st Flute	2 — 2nd F Horn	*available for download from*
5 — 2nd Flute	2 — 1st Trombone	*www.alfred.com/supplemental*
2 — Oboe	2 — 2nd Trombone	E♭ Alto Clarinet
2 — Bassoon	2 — 3rd Trombone	E♭ Contra Alto Clarinet
4 — 1st B♭ Clarinet	2 — Euphonium	B♭ Contra Bass Clarinet
4 — 2nd B♭ Clarinet	2 — Euphonium T.C.	1st E♭ Horn
4 — 3rd B♭ Clarinet	4 — Tuba	2nd E♭ Horn
2 — B♭ Bass Clarinet	Percussion — 6 players:	1st Trombone in B♭ T.C.
2 — 1st E♭ Alto Saxophone	2 — Bells	2nd Trombone in B♭ T.C.
2 — 2nd E♭ Alto Saxophone	2 — Percussion 1	3rd Trombone in B♭ T.C.
2 — B♭ Tenor Saxophone	(Suspended Cymbal, Bass Drum)	1st Trombone in B♭ B.C.
2 — E♭ Baritone Saxophone	2 — Percussion 2	2nd Trombone in B♭ B.C.
3 — 1st B♭ Trumpet	(Mark Tree, Triangle)	3rd Trombone in B♭ B.C.
3 — 2nd B♭ Trumpet	2 — Timpani	Euphonium in B♭ B.C.
3 — 3rd B♭ Trumpet		Tuba in B♭ T.C.
		Tuba in B♭ B.C.
		Tuba in E♭ T.C.
		Tuba in E♭ B.C.
		String Bass

Alfred

Please note: Our band and orchestra music is collated by an automatic high-speed system. The enclosed parts are now sorted by page count, rather than score order.

Northern Lights

FULL SCORE
Duration - 3:50

By Yukiko Nishimura

© 2023 ALFRED MUSIC
All Rights Reserved including Public Performance

49984S

Scan to interact

poco rit.
Fls.
1
2
Ob.
Bsn.
Cls.
1
2
3
B. Cl.
A. Saxes.
1
2
T. Sax.
Bar. Sax.
ff
p
fp
poco rit.
Tpts.
1
2
3
Hns.
1
2
Tbns.
1
2
3
Euph.
Tuba
Bells
Perc. 1
f
mp
Perc. 2
Timp.
27
28
29
30

13

49984S

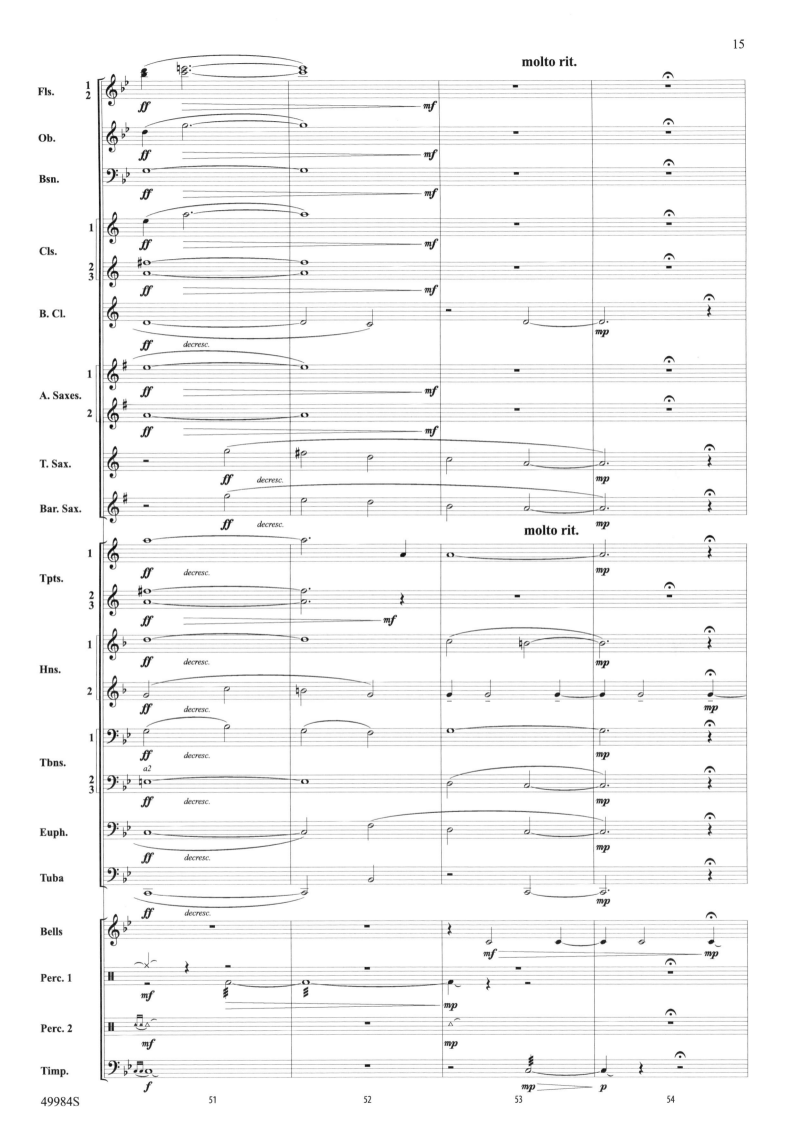

49984S